CW00722891

22-3

Dad

(n) Real life superhero by day, free taxi service by night.

See Also: Supertired

This edition published by Ravette Publishing 2019.

Ravette Publishing Limited
PO Box 876, Horsham, West Sussex RH12 9GH
info@ravettepub.co.uk

ISBN: 978-1-84161-410-6

Printed and bound in India by Replika Press Pvt. Ltd.

Dad

(n) Often overlooked, overlooked, underappreciated, (but much loved) parental figure.

URBAN WORDS

ℛℛ
RAVETTE PUBLISHING

Handsome

(adj) Good-looking, charming and in possession of regular, pleasing and most attractive features.

Dad

(n) Someone to look up to no matter how tall you get.

URBAN WORDS

Father

(n) Killer of spiders and teller of bad jokes.
(See also ATM)

Chauffeur

(n) Your Dad.

Wheels On The Bus

(s) A song that ALL Dads know the words to.

Alcohol

(n) A bitter tasting fluid that makes Dads think they can dance.

URBAN
WORDS

Petrolhead

(n) A person who is excessively interested in or who is devoted to their car.

Insanity

(n) A hereditary disease that you get from your children!

Dad

(n) A Son's first hero, a Daughter's first love.

Beard

(n) A food storage device found on awesome men's faces.

Mantrum

(n) The childish rage displayed by a grown man when he doesn't get his own way.

I think so

(phr) I want to say yes, but don't want to be held accountable if the answer is no.

Walking Dad

(n) An overworked Super-Dad that feeds on chocolate and survives on caffeine.

URBAN WORDS

Bank

(n) Money providing leather item usually found in dad's pocket.

URBAN WORDS

Embarrassment

(n) A feeling that comes over you when Dad gets up to dance.

Eternity

(n) The last two minutes of a football game.

Daddy

(n) Giver of the best hugs and your very own Superhero.

Remote Control

(n) TV channel changing device which appears to be glued to a Father's hand.

URBAN WORDS

Adult

(n) A person who has stopped growing at both ends and is now growing in the middle.

URBAN WORDS

D.I.Y.

(n) Disastrous renovation without professional training or assistance.

URBAN WORDS

Dad

(n) Strong role model with unending patience.

URBAN
WORDS

Barbeque

(n) When a woman buys the food, washes and chops the salad, marinates the meat, tidies away, and then a man stands in front of a fire and drinks beer.

Home

(n) Where your wi-fi connects automatically.

Nagivate

(v) What someone does from the passenger seat.

Argument

(n) A discussion that occurs when the woman is right, and continues until the man realises it.

URBAN WORDS

Style

(v) Something that Dad doesn't have.

Barn

(n) A special place that you think you may have been raised in - as this is what Dad asks every time you leave a door open.

Dad

(n) A man with pictures in his wallet where his money used to be.

Your Mum

(n) The best response to any question.